# WRITE ON TARGET

BY J.S. KNODELL

Copyright 2016 by Toem Books

All rights reserved.
No part of this publication may be reproduced,
stored in a retrieval system, or transmitted in any form
or by any means, electronic, photocopying, recording,
or otherwise, without the prior permission of the publisher.

ISBN - 978-4-908152-12-2

Toem Languages
2-18 Kita 2 Nishi 26,
26WEST Bld. 4F
Chuo Ward, Sapporo, Japan

www.to-em.com

For all inquiries or comments:
info@to-em.com
(011) 839-3771

# ABOUT THE BOOK

**Write on Target** was written to help students practice writing in a variety of forms. The book focuses on 5 areas of writing: essays, short stories, sentences, poetry, and reading comprehension questions. Students with a high level of English proficiency would probably benefit most from using this textbook, in particular high school-university students.

I developed the textbook for my upper-level students in Japan. It is therefore a book designed to improve the writing skills of this type of student. The main aspects of the book are:

- to practice organized writing through essays
- to develop an understanding of essay form and idea creation
- to practice various essay forms such as Cause & Effect, Process, Informative, and Personal
- to enhance creativity through short story writing and poetry
- to foster an interest in writing and reading by examining 4 simplified short stories
- to develop stronger vocabulary skills through writing practice using common words found on the TOEFL exam

Writing is challenging for anyone who has tried to do it well. Hopefully, this textbook can aid students and teachers to enjoy the process of writing because the skill of writing is useful throughout life. Happy writing...

**NOTE**: The reading book is sold separately from Write on Target. While it is possible to find the 4 short-stories by other means, the name of the book is

Outstanding Short Stories by Penguin Readers (ISBN: 1-408-27644-5)

# TABLE OF CONTENTS

**ESSAYS** ............................................................................................................................1

**HOW TO WRITE AN ESSAY** ...............................................................................................1

    Argumentative Essay ...............................................................................................4

    Cause and Effect Essay ............................................................................................5

    Comparative Essay ..................................................................................................6

    Informative Essay ....................................................................................................6

    Personal Essay .........................................................................................................6

    CLASSIFICATION ESSAY ............................................................................................7

    process ESSAY .........................................................................................................7

**READING COMPREHENSION** .........................................................................................61

**SUMMARY** ....................................................................................................................61

    The Man Who Could Work Miracles  *H. G. WELL* ...................................................63

    The Model Millionair *Oscar Wilde* ........................................................................64

    The Doll's House   *Katherine MansField* ...............................................................66

    Lord Montrago  W.Somerset Maugham .................................................................67

**MAKING SENTENCES** ....................................................................................................71

    Making Perfect Sentences 1 ...................................................................................72

    making Perfect Sentences 2 ...................................................................................73

    Making Perfect Sentences 3 ...................................................................................74

    Making Perfect Sentences 4 ...................................................................................75

    Making Perfect Sentences 5 ...................................................................................76

    making perfect sentences 6 ...................................................................................77

    Making Perfect Sentences 7 ...................................................................................78

    Making Perfect Sentences 8 ...................................................................................79

    Making Perfect Sentences 9 ...................................................................................80

    Making Perfect Sentences 10 .................................................................................81

| | |
|---|---|
| Making Perfect Sentences 11 | 82 |
| Making Perfect Sentences 12 | 83 |
| Making Perfect Sentences 13 | 84 |
| Making Perfect Sentences 14 | 85 |
| Making Perfect Sentences 15 | 86 |
| Making Perfect Sentences 16 | 87 |

## POETRY .................................................................................................................. 88

| | |
|---|---|
| NARRATIVE | 88 |
| LIMERICKS | 89 |
| CINQUAIN | 90 |
| HAIKU | 91 |
| FREE VERSE | 93 |

## SHORT STORIES ..................................................................................................... 95

| | |
|---|---|
| APPENDIX | 125 |

# ESSAYS

## HOW TO WRITE AN ESSAY

Think of writing an essay as your chance to show your knowledge on a specific topic in an organized and logical way. It is also a chance for writers to show they understand the topic or questions being discussed, and that they can present their ideas in a convincing way.

There are many ways to write an essay, but here is a general guide to writing most essays. If you believe that writing an essay is a process, then you can follow these 4 steps:

1. Think about the question. Do you understand exactly what it is asking you to do?

2. Research and/or plan your ideas to answer the question of the essay. This is the most difficult and important part, so it needs time.

3. Write the essay, usually using 4-5 paragraphs (Introduction, Bodies 1-3, Conclusion)

4. Re-read your essay. Does it make sense? Did you find grammar mistakes?

ESSAY STRUCTURE:

A five-paragraph essay can have a simple yet very clear structure:

**Paragraph 1** is the introduction. It has around 4 sentences. The first is a general idea on the topic. The second sentence is a more specific sentence about the topic, and the third is the main idea of your essay. This is called the thesis statement, and it guides your whole essay. What you write tries to support this idea. The last sentence explains your 3 supporting ideas that will prove your main idea.

**Paragraph 2** explains the first of the supporting ideas. I suggest it to be your 2$^{nd}$ strongest idea. For example, if you are writing an essay for or against wearing uniforms, and you use the idea of TIME as a body topic. In the body, you would give 2 or 3 reasons why students should (or shouldn't) wear a uniform focusing on the idea of time (i.e. save time in the morning not having to pick what to wear).

**Paragraph 3** uses the second supporting idea you wrote in the introduction. It is important to keep this order so you don't confuse the reader. I recommend that students use their weakest idea here. Again, if you are writing about uniforms, you could use the idea of Fashion here, and give 2 or 3 reasons to support the idea.

**Paragraph 4** uses the third of the supporting ideas. It is your strongest idea. Because it is the last idea the reader will look at, I always tell students to keep the best for last because this is what the reader might remember the most clearly.

**Paragraph 5** is the conclusion. It repeats your topic sentences. It finishes with a strong sentence that sums up your main point.

## INTRODUCTION

In the INTRODUCTION of your essay, there are a few ideas you need to write about.

First, try to start your essay strongly to catch your reader's interest and attention in the first sentence. Here are 3 ways to start an essay: A famous quote, an important statistic, or an interesting general statement about the topic.

Also, identify the purpose of the essay by telling the reader clearly what you are going to write about. This is called the THESIS STATEMENT.

Finally, have 1 sentence to explain how you will solve the purpose of your essay. These are the body topics. They are the issues you will examine in the essay, and can be ideas such as health, money, time, education, relationships, and society, etc.

## BODY

The body paragraphs develop your essay. In some cases, your essay will have 3 bodies that are logically linked together and flow into each other.

Each body has a focus, and a well-written body stays focused on the main idea.

Within the paragraph, try to use specific words that help the reader easily understand your thoughts. Here is a short list of these words:

| Furthermore | To begin | Nevertheless | Because |
| --- | --- | --- | --- |
| Also | Second | However | For that reason |
| In addition | Lastly | And yet | Therefore |
| Moreover | Finally | On the other hand | As a result |
| As well | For example, | In other words | Probably |
| In the same way | For instance | For example | Perhaps |
| Similarly | To demonstrate | To clarify | In fact |
| To begin | To summarize | In conclusion | To conclude |

BODY 1: USE THE 2ND BEST IDEA HERE.

Remember that it is the 1st idea you wrote in the introduction. Depending on the size of the essay, students should try to have 2-3 supporting ideas in each body. If you are using 2 ideas, then your paragraph should have at least 5 sentences:

The topic sentence: This introduces the topic of the paragraph

- First supporting idea
    ⇒ Example details that prove the idea
- Second supporting idea
    ⇒ Example or details that prove the idea

BODY 2: USE THE WEAKEST IDEA HERE.

Body 2 should be your weakest idea because it is hidden between the stronger ideas in your essay. It is written the same way as body 1.

BODY 3: USE THE BEST IDEA HERE.

I believe Body 3 should be your best idea because it is the last one the reader will look at, so it will leave an impression. By using your best idea here, you have a stronger chance of impressing the reader with your insight into the topic.

## CONCLUSION

In the conclusion, restate your goals and summarize what you wrote about. Explain why your ideas are important. Do not include new information in the conclusion.

## ARGUMENTATIVE ESSAY

**Argumentative essays not only give information but also explain an argument and try to convince the reader that your opinions are right. You need to be clear which side you support, usually either agreeing or disagreeing, but not both. Good argumentative essay topics have both pros and cons. Your main goal is to persuade the reader that your ideas are better than the other sides' arguments.**

## TOPICS

- Students don't need long vacations
- Athletes get paid too much money
- Smoking should be illegal
- Video games are harmful to people
- All zoos should be closed
- Public libraries are no longer needed
- Textbooks should be replaced with notebook computers
- Contact sports like boxing should be banned

## SAMPLE ESSAY – ARGUMENTATIVE

### PEOPLE SHOULD HAVE DOGS AS PETS

A famous American comedian once said that a dog is the only thing on Earth that will love you more than yourself (Josh Billings). For thousands of years, people have kept dogs as pets, and they are one of the most popular types of pets in the world. In this essay, I will explain why dogs make perfect pets for people of all ages. I will explain this by focusing on money, and education, and health.

People should own dogs as pets because of money. To begin, having a dog forces people to limit the amount of times they can go out. For example, dog owners have difficulty traveling overnight because they must take care of their dogs. As a result, they aren't able to travel much, and can save money. Also, dog owners help support other businesses. For example, dog food can cost owners thousands of dollars a year, and when a dog gets sick, medical bills can be expensive. Because of these two reasons, pet owners help support companies that make dog food, as well as vets who treat animals.

Secondly, people should have dogs as pets due to education. Dog owners must learn to be committed and dedicated to their pets. For example, these people must remember to feed their pets every day, and to walk them regularly. As a result, having a dog as a pet teaches people to be responsible. Furthermore, the children of dog owners can learn a valuable lesson about life and how precious it is. In most cases, pet dogs will die before other family members. Although it is extremely sad, a dog's death helps teach younger people that life is short, precious, and that all things eventually die.

Lastly, having a pet dog is beneficially to owners' health. First, dogs can act as a guardian in pet owners' homes. For example, if a thief tries to break into a dog owner's home, the dog will most likely bark and warn the owner of the danger. In an extreme case, the dog might even save the owner's life. In addition, dog owners need to walk their dogs regularly. In this case, the owner is forced to spend time outside, and this activity benefits the owner's health.

In conclusion, this essay explained why dogs make an excellent pet. Dog owners can save money and help the economy, they can learn important life lessons, and these pet owners can improve their health. Life can sometimes be challenging, but having a dog can make it a little better for many reasons.

## CAUSE AND EFFECT ESSAY

In a cause and effect essay, writers explain the causes (reasons) or the effects (results) of some event or situation. For example,

(1) What are the causes of water pollution (what makes water pollution happen)
(2) What are the effects of not sleeping enough (the results of this situation)

Think about a cause and effect essay about war. In type 1, you would look for the causes of war. In this type of essay, you could connect your ideas in order, especially if you are explaining 1 war in particular. In other words, what caused the war to happen.

In type 2, a cause and effect essay on war would explain the effects of a war, for example, you could discuss people's poor health (i.e. not enough medicine, food, hospitals…) caused by war.

In general, students write a 5 paragraph essay, with each Body paragraph focusing on one of the causes (or effects). In each Body paragraph, try to use 2-3 ideas to support the main idea.

### ESSAY TOPICS

- What are the causes and effects of over-population
- What are the causes and effects of bullying
- What are the causes and effects of divorce
- What are the causes and effects of taking extra classes outside of school or work
- What are the causes and effects of casinos or pachinko parlors

## COMPARATIVE ESSAY

The purpose of this essay is to show the similarities and differences between one or two subjects: 2 countries, 2 ideas, 2 machines, or about how 1 thing has changed from the past to the present (or future). In some essays, teachers will want students to discuss both similarities and differences. In a 5-paragraph essay, you could write 2 Bodies about similarities, and one about differences. Ideas you can consider for this essay are size, price, health, benefits, impact, reputation, use of time, etc.

### ESSAY TOPICS

- Being a student and working full-time
- Being blind and having sight

## INFORMATIVE ESSAY

An informative essay focuses on sharing information with your reader. For this reason, it's best to pick a topic you have knowledge about, and are interested in. This type of essay gives new or unknown information that the reader might not have. So, it is important to support your ideas with convincing evidence. Using websites, newspaper articles and journals would be an excellent way to support your ideas.

### ESSAY TOPICS

- How are insects important in the world
- How do forests influence our lives
- How are friends important in our lives

## PERSONAL ESSAY

Personal essays deal with topics directly related to your life: an event, a relative, a period of time when you were growing up. Your goal is to personalize the essay so that the reader can share and understand how the topic affected you. Details are important in personal essays, so descriptions are needed. For example, if your father was the topic of this essay, you wouldn't just write that he was a quiet, powerful figure in your family. You would describe a situation that showed these characteristics.

In this way, a personal essay paints a picture that helps the reader share your experience.

One more thing to remember about personal essays is that the goal of the personal essay is to explain change, or specifically, how the event or person or time changed your life.

ESSAY TOPICS

- What was your most important summer vacation
- How has one person or thing influenced your life
- What are your goals for the next few years

## CLASSIFICATION ESSAY

In a classification essay, we organize things into groups and give examples of things that each group has. For example, if you choose to write about schools, each of your Body paragraphs would focus on a different kind of school. Then, you would define what characteristics each school has, how they are unique or special.

ESSAY TOPICS

- Types of schools
- Types of computers

## PROCESS ESSAY

This kind of essay describes how something is done or how we can use something in a series of steps. This is the type of essay we use when we are explaining how to use a new machine, register for a class online, or reach some goal.

ESSAY TOPICS

- How to prepare for a test
- How to save money
- How to have a great vacation or party

## STUDENTS DON'T NEED LONG VACATIONS

# ARGUEMENT

## ATHLETES GET PAID TOO MUCH MONEY

# ARGUEMENT

## SMOKING SHOULD BE ILLEGAL

ARGUEMENT

VIDEO GAMES ARE HARMFUL TO PEOPLE

# ARGUEMENT

ALL ZOOS SHOULD BE CLOSED

ARGUEMENT

PUBLIC LIBRARIES ARE NO LONGER NEEDED

ARGUEMENT

## TEXTBOOKS SHOULD BE REPLACED WITH NOTEBOOK COMPUTER

ARGUEMENT

CONTACT SPORTS LIKE BOXING SHOULD BE BANNED

ARGUEMENT

## WHAT ARE THE CAUSES AND EFFECTS OF OVER-POPULATION

CAUSE & EFFECT

## WHAT ARE THE CAUSES AND EFFECTS OF BULLYING

CAUSE & EFFECT

WHAT ARE THE CAUSES AND EFFECTS OF DIVORCE

CAUSE & EFFECT

WHAT ARE THE CAUSES AND EFFECTS OF TAKING EXTRA CLASSES OUT SIDE SCHOOL OR WORK

CAUSE & EFFECT

## WHAT ARE THE CAUSES AND EFFECTS OF CASINOS OR PACHINKO PARLORS

CAUSE & EFFECT

## BEING A STUDENT AND WORKING FULL-TIME

COMPARE

BEING BLIND AND HAVING SIGHT

COMPARE

HOW ARE INSECTS IMPORTANT IN THE WORLD

INFORM

HOW DO FORESTS INFLUENCE OUR LIVES

INFORM

HOW ARE FRIENDS IMPORTANT IN OUR LIVES

INFORM

WHAT WAS YOUR MOST IMPORTANT SUMMER VACATION

PERSONAL

HOW HAS ONE PERSON OR THING INFLUENCED YOUR LIFE

PERSONAL

WHAT ARE YOUR GOALS FOR THE NEXT FEW YEARS

PERSONAL

## TYPES OF SCHOOLS

# TYPES OF COMPUTERS

CLASSIFY

## HOW TO PREPARE FOR A TEST

PROCESS

## HOW TO SAVE MONEY

PROCESS

## HOW TO HAVE A GREAT VACATION OR PARTY

PROCESS

# READING COMPREHENSION

There will be 4 short stories analyzed in this section. We will look at these short stories by examining different elements of literature.

Authors don't usually write a story without first planning what they will write. They make this plan by focusing on some elements or areas of story writing. It is important to remember that authors make writing choices for particular reasons. For example, in the Harry Potter books, Voldemort's name was selected for a specific reason. Vol de mort in French means to escape death, and this is what he does. His name is a clue or hint to his character. This is one way authors plan what they will write.

When we know how writers think and develop a story, it not only helps us understand stories more completely, but it can also help us enjoy the small details that all great stories have.

For more information on elements of literature, go to the appendix at the back of this book.

## SUMMARY

Writing summaries is a useful way to practice writing and is a useful tool in our academic and professional lives. A summary has 2 objectives. The first is to write, in your own words, the general ideas and plot of the reading. Second, you need to use precise language to explain the story in your own words. So, you might notice the challenge: You need to write in general while using specific language.

HOW TO SUMMARIZE A STORY

One difficulty in writing summaries is what to include, and what to leave out. Here are some helpful hints on how to summarize:

(1) Include the writer's name and the title in the 1st sentence

(2) At the beginning, write a sentence that explains the writer's main point. Try answering the question, "What's the story about?" Your 1 sentence answer should be the writer's main point.

(3) If the story has chapters, use them to divide your summary. If you are summarizing a short story, divide the story into parts or sections. Depending on how long your summary is, try to

write at least 1 sentence for each part. This way, your summary will include every area of the story.

(4) Remember you don't need to repeat everything in the reading. Select only the essential, important parts of the reading, and don't include the rest.

(5) Continuing #4, small details should usually be ignored.

(6) Don't write your opinions about the reading.

(7) And finally, don't copy the writer's words. If you decide to use the author's words, use quotation marks.

The reading comprehension section includes a summary of each story.

THE MAN WHO COULD WORK MIRACLES  *H. G. WELL*

**PART 1: P.1—8**

1. How does Fotheringay's belief in miracles change?

2. How do his friends at the inn react after he does his 1st miracle?

3. How is Fotheringay able to do miracles?

4. What examples are given to show Fotheringay's character (give at least 2 examples)?

5. Why does Fotheringay want to keep his power a secret?

6. How does his power affect the plot (give one example)?

7. Why might Mr. Maydig be a good person to talk to about miracles?

8. What evidence is given to demonstrate Mr. Maydig's personality?

**PART 2: P.8—13**

1. How is the 1st paragraph in this part different from others?

2. What impression is given to the reader when Mr. Maudig is described as "full of the sweetness of unlimited power"?

3. How does Fotheringay show his foolishness?

4. Also, how does he show great wisdom?

5. How does the setting add realism to the story?

*6.* What is the main theme in the story?

*7.* What is ironic about the main character?

*8.* What is the plot in the story?

**SUMMARY**

THE MODEL MILLIONAIR *OSCAR WILDE*

1. Describe the character of Erskine (At least 3).

2. Why does Alan Trevor like Erskine?

3. At this time, what are the attitudes towards the poor and the people painters know?

4. Hughie is poor, but what clues are given that show he is not so poor?

5. What does it mean "An artist's heart is in his head"?

6. What makes Alan laugh out loud? Explain.

7. Why is Hughie upset about giving the money to Baron Hausberg?

8. What is a major theme in the story?

## SUMMARY

## THE DOLL'S HOUSE  *KATHERINE MANSFIELD*

1. At this time, what are people's attitudes toward people of different class?

2. What is the doll's house a symbol of?

3. How do we know the Kelveys are aware of their position in society?

4. What prevents the Kelveys from being accepted?

5. What mood is created when reading about the Kelveys (p.41-42)?

6. How is the doll house used?

7. Why were the girls so happy after attacking the Kelveys?

8. How is Kezia different?

9. Why would the Kelveys be happy at the end?

10. What is the plot in this story?

**SUMMARY**

|  |
|--|

## LORD MONTRAGO   W.SOMERSET MAUGHAM

***PART 1: P.79—84***

1. What impression does the description of Dr Audlin give to the reader?

2. What kind of life did he have, and how did it affect him?

3. Describe Lord Montdrago's faults.

4. What power struggle do the two men have at the beginning, and why?

5. How is the atmosphere dark in the 1st half of the story?

6. Why are Dr. Audlin 's abilities?

7. Why does Dr. Audilin dislike his abilities?

8. How can Lord Mountdrago be charming? Give an example.

## PART 2: P.84—91

1. Describe Lord Mountdrago's problem.

2. What do his dreams tell the reader about his fears?

3. Why does Dr. Audlin keep silent after Lord Montdrago speaks?

4. What does Mountdrago mean when he says "I'm not the man of my dreams"?

5. What is the solution to Lord Mountdrago's problem (in his opinion)?

6. When did his dreams start, and how often does he get them?

7. What isn't Lord Mountdrago telling Dr. Audlin?

8. What is the setting in the story so far, and how does this affect the story?

## PART 3: P.91—97

1. How are Mountdrago and Griffiths different (at least 2 things)?

_____

2. What and had Mountdrago done to Griffiths, and why is it important where it happened?

_____

3. Why does Mountdrago get so upset about Dr. Audlin's advice?

_____

4. What does Mountdrago mean when he says "It's not my fault that I ruined him?"

_____

5. How does Dr. Audlin feel about Mountdrago's death?

_____

6. What "dark forces" is Dr. Audlin talking about on page 97?

_____

7. What frightens Dr. Audlin the most, and why?

_____

8. What is the plot in the story?

_____

9. How is the atmosphere in the story created (give at least 2 examples)?

_____

10. What theme is presented in this story?

_____

**SUMMARY**

# MAKING SENTENCES

## COMMON MISTAKES STUDENTS MAKE

Writing a perfect sentence might sound easy for some, difficult for others. But many students make common errors, often because in their language, the grammar pattern is either different or doesn't exist.

**Articles** – used before nouns, A, An, The give many students trouble, especially Proper Nouns like the names of Mountains, Lakes, Buildings and Planets.

**Third Person** – when using the personal pronouns he/she/it, many students forget to use S when they refer to their friend, a robot, or piece of pizza.

**Irregular verbs** – English becomes more difficult to master when using irregular verbs such as hit, begin, or bite in the past tense.

**Subject-verb Agreement** – in most cases, students have no trouble with this grammar form, but the exceptions are problematic. For example, when using ONE OF, the noun is plural and the verb is in the 3$^{rd}$ person (i.e. One of my FRIENDS HAS a helicopter).

## COMMON TOEFL WORDS

This section uses a list of common words used in a series of TOEFL tests. The goal of this section is to practice your writing skills, in particular, your ability to write a grammatically perfect sentence.

On each page, you will have a suggestion about writing the sentences. You can use these ideas to help you make sentences in fun, interesting, and creative ways.

Don't be afraid to use your dictionary to check for words you don't know. But after you know the meanings, write your own sentences. It's a good way for you to remember those words.

# MPS 1

## MAKING PERFECT SENTENCES 1

Make a sentence using each word listed below.

| | |
|---:|---|
| rebellion | |
| curse | |
| biology | |
| microscopic | |
| cyclone | |
| dichotomy | |
| dictate | |
| conductive | |
| conduct | |
| facsimile | |
| manufacture | |
| perfect | |
| uniform | |
| fortify | |
| geography | |

## MAKING PERFECT SENTENCES 2

Make a sentence using each word listed below.

| | |
|---:|---|
| telegram | |
| autograph | |
| hideous | |
| dialogue | |
| typical | |
| manage | |
| manual | |
| mature | |
| matriarch | |
| mediocre | |
| dismiss | |
| submit | |
| multiply | |
| nominate | |
| synonym | |

## MAKING PERFECT SENTENCES 3

Start each sentence with a gerund. For example, this sentence starts with a gerund (Waking): *Waking up early to bake cakes takes a lot of patience.*

| | |
|---|---|
| perch | |
| sympathy | |
| patriarch | |
| pedal | |
| transport | |
| ascend | |
| scribble | |
| potential | |
| consecutive | |
| consent | |
| subsequently | |
| contact | |
| contemporary | |
| attractive | |
| convene | |

## MAKING PERFECT SENTENCES 4

Try to rhyme within the sentences, for example, Waking up early to bake cakes takes a lot of patience.

| | |
|---|---|
| adventurous | |
| reverse | |
| convert | |
| vocal | |
| revoke | |
| contribute | |
| involve | |
| hazardous | |
| poverty | |
| manipulate | |
| misunderstood | |
| distribution | |
| influence | |
| role | |
| popularity | |

## MAKING PERFECT SENTENCES 5

Each sentence must be more than _____ words.

| | |
|---|---|
| recording | |
| interpreting | |
| observing | |
| foretelling | |
| balance | |
| sustain | |
| overwhelm | |
| contaminate | |
| independent | |
| advance | |
| superior | |
| perilous | |
| outlandishly | |
| comparatively | |
| intrinsically | |

## MAKING PERFECT SENTENCES 6

Start each sentence with a place (Next door, Many miles away, In my dog's ear)

| | |
|---|---|
| completely | |
| distort | |
| show | |
| accentuate | |
| promote | |
| tedious | |
| uncontrollably | |
| common | |
| essential | |
| rejection | |
| accumulation | |
| deletion | |
| production | |
| intensified | |
| narrow | |

# MAKING PERFECT SENTENCES 7

Start each sentence with a time (In the past, Before I sleep, Next year)

| | |
|---|---|
| maintain | |
| alter | |
| vast | |
| ancient | |
| dense | |
| deep | |
| conceal | |
| boost | |
| disrupt | |
| halt | |
| minimize | |
| exaggerate | |
| generate | |
| specialize | |
| shelter | |

# MAKING PERFECT SENTENCES 8

Start your sentences by describing how something happens (Quietly, with anger, Filled with fear)

| | |
|---|---|
| reject | |
| avoid | |
| consume | |
| barter | |
| grown | |
| eaten | |
| gathered | |
| vibrant | |
| thick | |
| remarkable | |
| luscious | |
| elude | |
| maintain | |
| develop | |
| exhibit | |

# MAKING PERFECT SENTENCES 9

Make each sentence a question.

| | |
|---:|---|
| disappoint | |
| rely on | |
| pain | |
| burden | |
| uplifting | |
| unfounded | |
| nonchalant | |
| distract | |
| principle | |
| magnify | |
| moan | |
| distrust | |
| infect | |
| riot | |
| plea | |

# MAKING PERFECT SENTENCES 10

Start your sentences with an adjective ending with ED (Worried, Confused, Excited)

| | |
|---|---|
| swim | |
| feed | |
| live | |
| reproduce | |
| consistent | |
| noticeable | |
| distinguished | |
| formidable | |
| decline | |
| cover | |
| prosper | |
| immense | |
| striking | |
| attractive | |
| plentiful | |

## MAKING PERFECT SENTENCES 11

Start your sentences with an adverb (Slowly, Carefully, Amazingly)

| | |
|---:|---|
| create | |
| enrich | |
| accelerate | |
| typify | |
| absurd | |
| remarkable | |
| arbitrary | |
| spot | |
| improvement | |
| elementary | |
| intrude | |
| occasion | |
| personal | |
| intricate | |
| orderly | |

## MAKING PERFECT SENTENCES 12

Finish writing the sentences in under 25 minutes.

| | |
|---|---|
| gratifying | |
| consistent | |
| ideal | |
| moderate | |
| minuscule | |
| isolate | |
| harvest | |
| on account of | |
| digest | |
| limited | |
| overwhelmed | |
| allocate | |
| identified | |
| smallest | |
| resilient | |

## MAKING PERFECT SENTENCES 13

Don't use the word "I" in any of your sentences

| principal | |
|---:|---|
| dramatic | |
| preserve | |
| assimilate | |
| condense | |
| erratic | |
| complex | |
| legitimate | |
| indispensable | |
| position | |
| freed | |
| transport | |
| observe | |
| probed | |
| dissect | |

# MAKING PERFECT SENTENCES 14

Use 1 adjective in each sentence: Opinion, Size, Age, Shape, Color, Nationality, Material

| | |
|---:|---|
| repell | |
| documented | |
| precise | |
| crucial | |
| comprehensive | |
| adverse | |
| advantageous | |
| fundamental | |
| practical | |
| expansion | |
| articulate | |
| switch | |
| discover | |
| attractiveness | |
| renew | |

## MAKING PERFECT SENTENCES 15

Start sentences from A to O. For example, the 1st sentence must begin with a word starting with A, the second sentence starts with a B word, etc.

| | |
|---|---|
| quantity | |
| callous | |
| mostly | |
| actually | |
| normally | |
| partially | |
| intolerable | |
| annoying | |
| intrusive | |
| unhealthy | |
| substantial | |
| exceptional | |
| mysterious | |
| tangible | |
| renowned | |

MAKING PERFECT SENTENCES 16

Make a short story with the list of words. Dr. Seuss did, so why not you?

|  | |
|---:|---|
| appeal | |
| incredible | |
| scenic | |
| exaggerate | |
| create | |
| enhance | |
| effort | |
| intriguing | |
| distinct | |
| impressive | |
| various | |
| indigenous | |
| frail | |
| early | |
| conserved | |

# POETRY

In this section, we will be learning about 5 different forms of poetry. There is no real definition to poetry, but just remember that poetry shows feelings in few words. It can be funny, sad, boring, or scary, but it is up to the poet to decide what the meaning of the poem is. Like a painter, your words are the paint. Sometimes it is difficult to understand a painting, but the good paintings are the ones that make people think. A famous writer once wrote, "If I read a book and it makes my body so cold no fire ever can warm me, I know that is po-etry;" and another talked about poetry this way: "Poetry is what makes me laugh or cry or yawn, what makes my toenails twinkle, what makes me want to do this or that or nothing."

## NARRATIVE

Narrative poem tells a story and can be about anything. Sometimes the poem's lines have a rhyming pattern. Sometimes they don't rhyme at all.

*When I saw the news today*
*I was shocked at the strange way*
*A monkey danced and sang a song*
*I didn't think my eyes were wrong*
*So, I got on a plane and went to the zoo*
*Paid $5 and ran to the place*
*Where that monkey lived with a friendly kangaroo*
*I couldn't believe the size of their space*
*When I saw the two animals sitting alone*
*In a little cage the size of a box*
*I decided to break the 3 locks*
*Picked up the 2 animals and took them home*

BY GUY MULLAH

## LIMERICKS

Limericks are poems with five lines with a special beat and rhyming pattern: Lines 1, 2 and 5 have 9 beats and the last words rhyme. Lines 3 and 4 have 6 beats and rhyme with each other.

*There once was an old man from Katmandu*

*Whose poor donkeys came down with the flu*

*In the valley, he passed*

*All the people they gasped*

*At the donkeys that were uddering "moo"*

LIMERICK BY SUE

## CINQUAIN

At the most basic level a cinquin is a five-line poem or stanza. Here are two variations.

Method

Line 1 - a one word title

Line 2 - a 2-word phrase that describes your title or you can just use two words

Line 3 - a 3-word phrase that describes an action relating to your title or just actions words

Line 4 - a 4-word phrase that describes a feeling relating to your topic or just feeling words

Line 5 - one word that refers back to your title

---

Line 1 - two syllables

Line 2 - four syllables

Line 3 - six syllables

Line 4 - eight syllables

Line 5 - two syllables

*Ketchup*

*A tomato*

*Put upon hamburgers*

*An incredibly tasty thing*

*Healthy?*

BY GUY MULLAH

## HAIKU

Japanese form of poetry. Form is 17 syllables in three lines with pattern: first line, 5 syllables; second line 7 syllables; third line, 5 syllables. Usually has nature themes.

**Haiku are**:

**Very short:** just three lines usually fewer than twenty syllables long.

**Descriptive:** most haiku focus sharply on a detail of nature or everyday life.

**Personal:** most haiku express a reaction to or reflection on what is described.

**Divided into two parts:** as they read haiku aloud, students should find that each includes a turning point, often marked by a dash or colon, where the poet shifts from description to reflection, or shifts from close-up to a broader perspective.

**Form:** Traditional Japanese haiku have seventeen syllables divided into three lines of five syllables, seven syllables, and five syllables respectively. These syllable counts are often ignored when haiku are written in other languages, but the basic form of three short lines, with the middle line slightly longer than the other two, is usually observed.

**Structure:** Haiku divide into two parts, with a break coming after the first or second line, so that the poem seems to make two separate statements that are related in some unexpected or indirect way. In Japanese, this break is marked by what haiku poets call a "cutting word." In English and other languages, the break is often marked by punctuation. This two-part structure is important to the poetic effect of a haiku, prompting a sense of discovery as one reads or a feeling of sudden insight.

**Language:** Haiku should include what Japanese poets call a *kigo* -- a word that gives the reader a clue to the season being described. The kigo can be the name of a season (autumn, winter) or a subtler clue, such as a reference to the harvest or new fallen snow. Through the years, certain signs of the seasons have become conventional in Japanese haiku: cherry blossoms are a kigo for spring, mosquitoes a kigo for summer. Sometimes, too, the kigo will refer to an individual moment in the natural cycle, such as dawn or moonrise, without refer-ence to a particular season. The kigo is also important to the haiku's effect, anchoring the experience it describes in a poetic here and now that helps sharpen the imaginative focus.

**Subject:** Haiku present a snapshot of everyday experience, revealing an unsuspected significance in a detail of nature or human life. Haiku poets find their subject matter in the world around them, not in ancient legends or exotic fantasies. They write for a popular audi-ence and give their audience a new way to look at things they have probably overlooked in the past.

HAIKU EXAMPLES

*When the first flake falls*

*Land below is green and warm*

*But it won't last long*

ANTON KISSMATE – MOSCOW, RUSSIA

*From dust to dust*

*In dust I move breathlessly*

*Sunlight revealing all*

NATALIE LESAGE- SALMON ARM, BC, CANADA

*Blowing from the west*

*Leaves meet to discuss their fate*

*Lovers must part ways*

ALEXANDER BAMBA - KEY WEST, FL, USA

*Hitchhiking at night*

*The moon reaches to tell me*

*I am not alone*

TOMA OKUYAMA – SAPPORO, JAPAN

## FREE VERSE

Free verse is just what it says it is - poetry that is written without proper rules about form, rhythm, meter, etc.

*Outside at night*

*I can hear him walking*

*Along the street, around the corner*

*Up the stairs, into my home*

*His cookies are waiting,*

*Our tree greets him silently*

*Then he is gone to the house next door*

*I can still hear him*

(WINTER POEM BY GUY MULLAH)

# SHORT STORIES

HOW TO WRITE SHORT STORIES?

The most important part of writing a short story is the problem. There must be a conflict in the story that the main character must solve. The story must be believable to the readers, and it must challenge and surprise the readers to keep them inter-ested in the story. The ending of the story is also very important because that is what the reader is reading last, so that is what most readers will remember about the story. Have fun, and you must be interested in writing the story, or else the reader will be bored.

5 ELEMENTS OF A STORY

## The Plot

The plot is the outline to your story. It is the main problem/problems in your story. Usually, stories have a good and bad guy with conflicts between the two that try to fix the problems you have created. Good stories have a protagonist (good guy) who is weaker than the antagonist (bad guy), but somehow, the protagonist defeats the antagonist (usually, but not always). If you think about Harry Potter and Voldemort, this is a good example of how a weaker protagonist defeats a stronger antagonist. How can a small, weak, unskilled Potter defeat the stronger, scarier Voldemort? Harry does this by using his friends, inner strength, and unknown skills to win out over the powerful Voldemort. Give your stories lots of problems and twists, and then at the end, solve the prob-lems in a believable way. Please remember that the ending of your story should be surprising. Most great short stories or movies have an ending that leaves the reader thinking "Wow!". In the last Harry Potter book, I was very shocked when I read that one of the main characters dies. This is the kind of ending that readers remem-ber. You don't have to kill everybody, but leave the reader with the feeling that something unexpected has hap-pened, and probably that will be a good ending.

## The Setting

The setting is the time and place in the story. When and where your story happens is very important because this is the picture of where the action happens, and it changes the feel of your story. If it takes place on the moon, in a forest, or on top of a mountain, the picture of the setting always affects how the reader feels about your story. The time of your story is also important because of the technology that will exist at that time. For example, these days, people travel in airplanes, have

TVs, and use guns. Five hundred years ago, these things did not exist. Describing the setting in your story will make it feel more real to the reader.

## The Theme

The theme in the story is what the writer tries to teach the reader. These are ideas that you have that allow you to tell your story for a reason. Do you want to tell your reader that, like Harry Potter, having good friends in your life is very important? Or that even if you are facing a difficult time, never give up? The theme is the idea that you want to teach your reader, and this helps you stay focused on your story.

## The Mood

This is the feeling in your story. Is your story scary, funny, serious, very exciting, or a combination of them all? If you know what kind of story you want to write, then you can choose the types of words you will use in your story. For example, if it is a scary story, you will probably use words like DARK, TERRIBLE, SILENTLY, CLOUDY…Often, the weather, colours, or even people's names can be used to create a mood in the story. Knowing the mood, you want helps you stay focused on the kind of story you want to write.

## The Characters

The characters are the people, animals, or objects doing the action in your story. Good characters have charac-teristics that all people have, like fear, love, and hate. You should try to make a picture of the characters with your words. For example, you could say, "Michael was a tall boy with short black hair, a round chubby face, and he always wore pink shirts." Write a picture of the characters so that the reader can imagine who he or she is, and this makes the story feel more real. Also, the names of the characters are often important because it gives a clue as to who that character is. Joe Simple tells the reader that Joe is not the smartest guy in the world, and Mary Butcher might not be a very nice girl. Talking about the characters' clothes, body, habits, and personality only make the story believable, and that is one goal of writing stories.

### WRITING SHORT STORIES

Short stories should have the 5 basic elements explained above. Before you start writing your story, take some time and plan out the kind of story you want to write. It will only make it better. Also, don't forget your commas, periods, quotation marks, use verbs in the past tense, indent your paragraphs, and have fun using your great imagination to make a fantastic story. Good luck!

## STORY TITLES

Story titles are very important for short stories because it is the first impression that readers get from stories. Some readers decide to read a book by just looking at the story titles.

1. The Banana Republic

2. The Company

3. The Fall

4. Sand

5. The Forgotten People

6. King Klumsy

7. The Follower

8. The Salesman

9. The Blue Notebook

10. Crash

11. Why Me?

12. Mourning and Knight

### SHORT STORIES SUGGESTIONS

For each story, you will have a suggestion about writing the story. These suggestions can help you think of different ways to start or end your story, give you ideas on how to develop your characters or plots, and can suggest a variety of writing techniques to make your stories (hopefully) better.

For example, in story #1 The Banana Republic, the suggestion is about the last sentence in the story. Some writers like to think about the ending first to help guide them to the conclusion. If you want, change the suggested last sentence, but try the technique.

**Story Title: The Banana Republic**

Suggestion - The last sentence in the story is "They never spoke to each other again."

SHORT STORY I

**Story Title: The Company**

Suggestion - Use only 3 quotes in the story. This will make the quotes stand out in your story.

# SHORT STORY 2

**Story Title: The Fall**

Suggestion - Think of a theme you want to write about, and focus on that in the story, such as a story about a person in need. The person meets someone who can help, but at a very high cost. The theme here could be how much are people willing to sacrifice to reach their goals?

SHORT STORY 3

**Story Title: Sand**

Suggestion - A story with only 2 characters, told in the 1st person narrative ("I was driving my car when I saw a woman standing by the side of the road.")

**Story Title: The Forgotten People**

Suggestion - A story with a surprising ending ("The two of them realized why nobody was talking to them. They were ghosts and not a part of this world anymore.")

SHORT STORY 5

**Story Title: King Klumsy**

Suggestion - Start with a description of the setting (Her room was like a sauna. The windows were closed, the heat on full, and Jane was lying in bed, covers over her head. She was wearing her thick winter jacket and shivering.)

SHORT STORY 6

**Story Title: The Follower**

Suggestion - Start your story in the middle of a conversation

**SHORT STORY 7**

**Story Title: The Salesman**

Suggestion - Start your story with a thought from a character in your story (Don't ask me, please don't ask me. I sat at the back of the classroom, hiding behind Big Mike, hoping that Ms. Larsen wouldn't pick me.)

SHORT STORY 8

**Story Title: The Blue Notebook**

Suggestion - •Start your story with a surprising/shocking statement (When I was a child, I used to put dead bugs into my brother's soup.)

**Story Title: Crash**

Suggestion - Start your story with a simile or metaphor (His room was messier than a city after a tornado passed through it.)

**Story Title: Why Me?**

Suggestion - Start your story with a question (How would you feel if your best friend was trying to steal your girlfriend, and everyone knew about this except you?)

# SHORT STORY II

**Story Title: Mourning and Knight**

Suggestion - Give your main character(s) some Idiosyncrasies. These are little habits or movements or actions that people do. For example, some people scratch when they don't know an answer. Other people sweat a lot when nervous.

SHORT STORY 12

# APPENDIX

## ELEMENTS OF LITERATURE

Allegory – A story in which the characters represent some human characteristic (i.e. evil, honesty, or bravery). This kind of story tries to show some larger lesson or meaning to life.

Character - A character in a story can be an animal, a person, or a thing that is involved in the story. There are many types of characters writers can use, but

in most cases, stories have a protagonist and antagonist.

Conflict - The struggle and problems that exist between characters in a story.

Diction – The word choice of the writer that helps develop themes, atmosphere, character, etc.

Imagery - The author's attempt to create a mental picture in the mind of the reader. Imagery uses sensory language to describe taste, touch, sight, smell, and sound.

Plot – Events within a story can follow a pattern, the telling of the story.

Narrator / Point of View - Who tells the story and how it is told. If the narrator is involved in the story's action, we call this a first-person narrative. A story told by a voice not in the story is a third-person narrative.

Plot – Events within a story can follow a pattern, the telling of the story.

Setting - The place or time of the action. The setting provides the historical and cultural background for characters.

Symbolism - When an object has a deeper meaning, and means more than itself.

Theme - The message, 'big idea', or teaching in a story. In other words, what the writer is trying to tell the reader about life.

Tone / Mood / Atmosphere - the feeling in the story created by using, for example, certain diction (words), setting, and other ways to convey emotions onto the reader.

**Grading Rubrics for Short Stories and Short Essays**

**Short Story Grading Sheet**     TOTAL: /20

| | |
|---|---|
| Does the story have a beginning, middle, end? | /2 |
| Is the grammar perfect/average/weak? | /2 |
| Is the spelling perfect/average/weak? | /2 |
| Is it easy to understand the problem in the story? | /2 |
| Is the problem in the story fixed at the end? | /2 |
| Is the ending of the story interesting/surprising? | /2 |
| Does the writer describe the setting? | /2 |
| Does the writer use past tense verbs? | /2 |
| Is the writing clear/easy to read? | /2 |
| Does the story have many problems? | /2 |

**Essay Grading Sheet**     TOTAL: /20

| | |
|---|---|
| Does the essay have 5 paragraphs? | /1 |
| Does the introduction explain the body topics? | /1 |
| Do the body paragraphs introduce the main idea in the 1st sentence? | /5 |
| Does the introduction clearly state the goal of the essay? | /3 |
| Do the ideas have strong explanations? | /3 |
| Is the grammar good? | /1 |
| Does each idea in the body have 2 sentences? | /3 |
| Does the introduction start with an interesting sentence? | /1 |
| Do you believe the essay proved its point clearly? | /1 |
| Does the conclusion repeat the topic and the body ideas? | /1 |

www.ingramcontent.com/pod-product-compliance
Lightning Source LLC
Chambersburg PA
CBHW080414170426
43194CB00015B/2810